Gabriel's Beach

....

HAGIOS
PRESS

Gabriel's Beach

....

Neal McLeod

HAGIOS PRESS
Box 33024 Cathedral PO
Regina, Saskatchewan S4T 7X2
www.hagiospress.com

Library and Archives Canada Cataloguing in Publication

McLeod, Neal
  Gabriel's beach / Neal McLeod.

Poems.
Includes some text in Cree
ISBN 978-0-9783440-5-4

  1. McLeod, Neal – Family – Poetry. 2. Vandall, Gabriel – Poetry. 3. Cree Indians – Poetry. I. Title.

PS8625.L46G32 2008   C811'.6   C2008-905277-3

Edited by Allan Safarik.
Designed and typeset by Donald Ward.
Cover art: *Gabriel's Beach* by Neal McLeod.
Cover design by Yves Noblet.
Set in Futura Light BT.
Printed and bound in Canada.

The publishers gratefully acknowledge the assistance of the Saskatchewan Arts Board, The Canada Council for the Arts, and the Cultural Industries Development Fund (Saskatchewan Department of Culture, Youth & Recreation) in the production of this book.

these words are dedicated
to all of the men
who have held
the fire from Gabriel's beach
and to all our grandmothers
whose strength
helped us survive

kinanâskomitin Tasha, for helping a lost son
find his way home

Contents

Foreword

So many sad and painful events mar the family histories of Aboriginal people that often heroes like Gabriel get lost in the darkness of memory. We are fortunate in our family not only to have stories of this wonderful old man, but also to be able to say we knew him personally.

There are no great uncles in our culture; all our old people are *mosôms* and *kôhkoms*. It is a way to bind kinship and show respect. Gabriel was my generation's *mosôm*. He was our granny's brother, someone we loved and admired and who always had time to take us fishing, tell us a story about a far-away place, or just wipe away a tear.

He was a *môsâpêw*, who had taken a vow as a young man never to marry but, rather, to serve his people. In olden times, there were such men and women, people who took this vow to devote their lives to becoming a particular kind of healer, warrior, storyteller, or person. They placed great importance on mentoring young people, and *mosôm* Gabriel did this for many of us. He spent hours telling us stories and teaching us about the protocols and responsibilities associated with them. His vow brought love and honour to his family and to his country, and it lit the way for my generation's journey into a new place in the world. Thank you, Neal, for honouring him with this beautiful book.

Maria Campbell
Gabriel's Crossing, Saskatchewan
Summer 2008

Acknowledgements

I would like to thank my father, Jeremiah McLeod, and my uncle, Burton Vandall, for telling me the stories of *mosôm* Gabriel. I would like to thank Allan Safarik, Paul Wilson, and Tasha Beeds for their editing of the text.

In my work, I always strive to include the use of the Cree language, and would like to thank Arok Wolvengrey for his editing of the Cree text and the creation of the glossary.

I would like also to thank Don Ward for his typesetting, which creates a beautiful space for the poems to dwell in.

Introduction

My grandfather, Gabriel Vandall, had a profound influence on the men in my family. My father, Jerry McLeod, and my uncle, Burton Vandall, often told stories of our mosôm Gabriel. mosôm Gabriel's strength, bravery, and character were concretely embodied in the stories, which spoke of his experiences of war. I heard these stories growing up and I understand his life as an extension of the ideals of the okihcitâwak ("worthy men") from kayâs (long) ago. Despite the ravages of colonialism that both my people and our traditional lands have experienced, we still have dignity and strength.

mosôm Gabriel had a strong genealogy: his life and body were at the crossroads of powerful trajectories of history and collective memory. His uncles had struggled against the encroaching colonial presence of the British and the Canadians, and were independent and strong people. Gabriel's mother, cîhcam, resisted the new order that was put upon the land. She practiced traditional medicine, and left a legacy that many of her grandchildren continue to draw on. This strength, which they epitomized, allowed people to survive difficult times.

On one level, Gabriel's beach tells the story of Juno Beach in 1944, where nimosôm landed and experienced some of the heaviest fighting on the Western Front. It was on this beach, where many of his friends and comrades died, that he dug into the bank of ancestral memory to find the strength to bring the sky back from the water. For this ability, he was a highly respected soldier. It is the fire of Gabriel's beach, which affirms life and which illustrates cultural vitality.

On another level, Gabriel's beach represents violence in a wider, historical sense. The events of 1885 changed the life and land of Indigenous people in a profound way. The prophecies of the iron rope across the land came to be fulfilled; the land was cut up into grids to suite colonial fantasies of what the west should be. The Saskatchewan River, *kisiskâciwani sîpiy*, which had once given so much life to Indigenous people, was now lost. It was lost to a new order, its name muted in the English language. We, as Indigenous people and as Indigenous men, also became lost in the wake of the changes that occurred. We were once *okihcitâwak*: hunters, providers, and soldiers. But when the river of our ancestral dreams was lost, we, too, become lost.

I thank my *mosôm* Gabriel for teaching us that the fire of the beach helps us to survive and keep us from surrendering, but, in my own life, I have been a son of a lost river, unable to hold the fire of Gabriel's beach. I have struggled to understand my own masculinity in an environment which has often been violent. I also acknowledge how, in my life, I have created violence.

Through women such as Grandmother *cîhcam* and the late Beatrice Lavallee, however, Indigenous men like me have been able to find our way home. These women provided word maps, and gave us the stories to help us find our way back to the river, and back to our language and culture. I thank all my grandmothers for providing a cool wind on my hands to give me the grace and the wisdom to hold this fire.

With the stories and the strength of our ancestors, we can find our home in the river again. With love, we can create beautiful images in the eternal flow of water and creation. It is my ancestors, my sons, Glen, Cody, and Justin, as well as my step-son Dakota, and my beautiful Tasha, with whom I connect in love, who make up the flow of deep, richly blue, forever-turning waters.

Neal McLeod
Peterborough, Ontario
Summer 2008

Dreaming on Gabriel's Beach

....

SLEEPING ON GABRIEL'S BEACH

my body knows no rest
I sleep no more
unrest moves me
without end
my eyes cannot close the sky

I grow tired of trying
to pull together
moments that no longer
fit together
I grow tired of holding fire
grow old, crack
fall from my body

the only place
I can sleep
Gabriel's beach
metal bodies
and flesh bodies
torn open
to the wind and skies

I sleep in this gutted tomb
my body
feels warm water
rush over me
I feel the pain pass away
for a moment

exploding shells
become stars
my eyes close the sky

MOSÔM GABRIEL'S UNIFORM

mosôm wore his uniform
metals marked
places of ocean
capped white
sky heavy
with falling metal
unable to find
the end of ocean

his feet marked light
in the dark places
without end to reach

"He fought for his people"
they said
spoke of the pits
where they kept him
they say his mind
"floated above the water"
lost at sea
torn from parklands
unable to be heavy
in deep blue

floating to the bottom
of deep water, *timikamîhk*
not light enough
to journey back
into the sky

GABRIEL'S BEACH

last night I dreamt
of Gabriel's beach
Juno Beach
where thunder met
the water

short hollow breaths
coughed up sand
felt water crash against me
through the stretch of my soul

friend hit by loosened shell
head falls from body frame
bursts like ripe summer berry
upon his uniform
mosôm Gabriel
said it was
the only warm thing
he felt that day

ripping water skin
artillery cutting
smoke fragments
spread of the sky
cuts of sky
in his body
cold hollow breaths
hands sweat
flashes of rolling hills
parkland forests
through his mind

thunderbirds from the sky
unable to find
the edge of water
some panic, grab
hands of empty water
without form

sounds of German shredders
bring him back
to bloodied beach
thick with rage, smoke
quiet bodies
hungry *wîhtikow*
feeds on fallen bodies

dry through my lungs
in deep darkness
I felt a fire
burn through me
ati-pihkopayinwa nicihciya
my hands turn to ash
I could feel no more
nikî-waniskân
I awoke
coughed sand
from Gabriel's beach
lost myself
in still eternity

THE SHREDDERS

they called
the German machine gunners
"shredders"
they cut bodies
with piercing bullets
like *wîhtikow* teeth

the shredders
like snakes
pulling the thunderbirds
deeper into the water
no chance
to dream like old men
only kill
young men's dreams

TIGERS

sand soaked with fresh blood
men fell from hidden shredders
sand thrown from boots
they took them out
and made a beachhead
many friends lay silent
empty of words and breath

Gabriel saw the Tigers piercing
thin roof and walls of armour
"housed the people inside," he said
inside, fire through them
short, hollow breaths
closed in, darkness came

mosôm Gab welded pieces
ê-kî-akohkasikêt
of metal on tanks
thicker walls
thicker roofs
to protect the ones
"housed inside," he said
metal from bulldozers
patched together
like rainbow *nôhkom's* quilt
Tigers had to bite harder
shredders had to shred harder
Gabriel turned the darkness
of bloody sand
into a quiet hard stillness

DREAMING BEACH

I live by a lake now
see the water
moving slowly
catching the sky
in small pieces
moving it toward me

dreaming beach
along the water
hitting the shore lightly
feet full of sand
between toes
skin heavy and dry

passing sun
sky moving to orange
lapping water
scatters pieces of
sand iridescent
beneath my feet

only the *mêmêkwêsiwak*
keep sand bodies
to heal us
as the earth turns cold

DREAMING THE SKY

hill boss
sitting on a throne
with inscriptions on it
in front of rubble
not quite pictures
he was bald
surrounded by arbour
squared, not quite writing
flames on it, his helper
pointing to the distance

where they keep
coming more and more
sky turning completely white
waiting for it
to crash upon us
boss getting more desperate
made the world hotter
flames licking the sky and earth
another protector of the area
beginning to melt, statue
I urge him to move
to free himself
make himself flesh again
he could not
the other helper
turning into a bird
protecting me from the bullets
chasing the boss
the bird threw pieces of the sky
hitting and crushing him
like a pumpkin
giving me a path to flee

HILL DREAM

from open water
approached, blackened spaces
ripples, shreds of grey on moving
blue water
black outlines
closer to water
brought out ochre
of the sand

we ran away
from their approach
sheltered from the heavy sky
which became red and orange
waiting for thunderbirds
wooden building
covered our approach
splintered and fractured
inside the church
syllabics on walls
more like drawings
than writings
saw the glass over
the crucifix
"will probably crack"
I thought
pieces holding moon's light
in their shattering descent

wooden spaces watched through spaces
seeing them come closer
mouth wide open like *wîhtikowak*

YOUR LIGHT

my soul
hollowed out
by darkened sun
deep nights
water beings
unable to swim
to the surface

your light *sâpowâstêw*
from the surface
softens the nights
opens the blackness to spaces
where I can swim again

YOUR BODY IS MY BEACH

my feet grab the pieces
of sand
brushes against
the stretch of toes
dig small pieces of myself
make tracks
membrane *kahkiyaw waniskâwak askîhk*
waking earth
iskoyikohk itê ê-kanawâpahtamân
as far as I look
beach stretches
belt of sanded work
patterned with deep blue of sky
light blue of ocean
a beaded belt

your body is my beach
where I bury the bullets
of Gabriel's beach
upon the shore
sanded flesh calmed by
insistent water brings deep ocean
your body is the beach
of my dreams
and keeps paths
for my body to return
and to calm the fire
of dreams of deep darkness

MOSÔM GABRIEL CAPTURED

water in all directions
unknown latitude
filled with blood
turned by shouts
into the spray of shredders

Gab went too far
on the other side
of the hill
they had passed
the shredders
hidden in nests
snakes waiting to bite
filling the beach with
bullets and shells
Germans surrounded them

hunger made them crazy
stomachs empty
vessels without holding
they think *wîhtikow* thoughts
eat their own excrement
to survive Gab speared mice
as he lay in the pit

NAMES

slow, his voice
like an old jazz singer
deep, a little crackly
like spring creatures
calling each other

iskotêw, fire, his grandfather
the father of *côhcam*
ran high in forests
taken down by a grizzly bear
Burns, *iskotêw*

cikôsiw, French Man
from Shoal Lake, Red Earth
wore the old fashioned hat

napocokan
crooked hips
Bernard Constant
holds his name
stayed at The Pas
father was from Montreal

nîkân-isi, "the foremost one"
the first McLeod, thunderbird
brings the sky to the water
at Gabriel's beach

names, our speaking bodies,
help us find our way
home to the lost river

MOSÔM PÂCINÎS

mosôm pâcinîs
was the grandson
of old Joseph Vandall
who died at Batoche
pâcinîs led his people
in the summer
with his old beaver hat
his old mosôm hat
with ruffles in the middle
led them like
an old buffalo captain

with names and places
he gives form
to the moment of my birth
pâcinîs traveled
made his way
after the times of the troubles
ê-mâyahkamikahk
his mother was cîhcam
Maria Vandall, born daughter of masaskâpaw
touches the bottom of the water
like name strands
touching the bottom of water
as sleeping grandfathers awake

MOSÔM JOHN R. McLEOD

he always wore his pants up high
past his belly over his paunch
opakwahtêhon ê-ispipitahk
roll back tobacco
thick fingers struggle
find precision
bits of tobacco spill on the table
vogue papers
red image on ochre
Indian Affairs heavy glasses
would today be strangely trendy
he was serious, focused
like a Sgt. in the army
offered me moose nose
and other Indian delicacies
always cooked tubs of bannock
deep fried
gave them to old people
when we went to powwows
after he died
I lost the hoka
and never went back
I dreamt of him
in gold clothing
he told me of the other side
of the sky

KÊTAHTAWÊ Ê-KÎ-TAPASÎT

wîhtikôhkân
was not a Christian
unlike his brother *mostos*
he was a swashbuckler
a traveller
one of his grandfathers
came from Montreal
Xavier became Janvier
turns of names
and languages
like the Saskatchewan River
around hills and trees

back in the long ago
kayâs time
marriages were planned
families connected
through younger ones
wîhtikôhkân had a pre-arranged marriage
he came south from Cold Lake

he went into the church
to meet his wife
walked up the aisle
pews were full
chatter becomes still
she took down her veil
êkwa mâmâsîs ê-osîhiht
but she was made poorly
kêtahtawê ê-tapasît
he fled quickly
and found another wife

JESUS

one time they invited *wîhtikôhkân*
to sing in the church
he brought his drum
but they were singing
a different kind of song
songs about Christian soldiers
scratched out in Cree syllabics
Cree voices
stretching to say these names

another time
he was sitting
in the church
and this man was preaching
about fire and hell
eternal damnation
sâh-sîhcisiwak
they were sitting tight
packed in the pews

wîhtikôhkân used to smoke
his little pipe
with his hat on
and listen to the words
religion and stories
of the newcomers
the people that his brother *kinosêw*
made the deal with
he said, he couldn't understand why
they would talk about Jesus
when they killed him
he used to think
they were afraid
they would be punished

1885, BATOCHE

mosôm Gabriel
was my grandfather
cîhcam was his mother
his father and four brothers
had fled west
from the British soldiers' march
in 1870

some of *mosôm* Gab's relatives
had fought in 1885
ê-mâyahkamikahk they said
"where it went wrong"
along the *kisiskâciwani-sîpiy*
by Batoche
they sent the young people away
old men fought
told jokes, teased, chided
each other
as bullets cut
bodies into the earth

buried outside the graveyard
unsanctioned by sacred sanctuary
another of Gabriel's grandfathers
general with Napoleon
seems soldiering was in the blood

1885, CUTKNIFE HILL

Red Coats
change the colour
of early spring
horses and men
wake sleeping clumps
of clay and earth
the red forms
approach the Crees

two *môhcw-âyak*
crazy ones
go ahead and play
dance and taunt
approaching lines
of British Empire

large opening
tunnel carved into
the side of a hill
shelter sought
Red Coats' lines
sewed by *okihcitâwak* hands
women pleaded
"If you fight
they will come back
with more and get even.
We will have to deal
with the consequences."
my dad told me this story
of Cutknife Hill

MASKIHKIY ASTOTIN

as *iskotêw*, the original Burns
passed through Alberta
he picked up this story
of *maskihkiy astotin*
Medicine Hat
land full of gas and words

Blackfoot blackened
out Cree footsteps
surrounded, cut off all paths
beside the river they moved
up against banks
like a boxer on the ropes
kâ-mônahihkos, Digging Weasel
had a pretty daughter
nipahi-miyosit
terribly beautiful

Blackfoot took to words
with guns loaded
river pushed down the sky
the Blackfoot leader said,
"We will leave you alone
If you let me have your daughter."
"*môya*. No. You cannot have her,"
the chief said
he loved her too much

he threw his bonnet
in the river
and it was called
maskihkiy astotin
Medicine Hat
Crees went to their camp
along the river
nêhiyawak in the camp
began to wonder what would happen
ispîhk ê-wî-pê-sâkâstêk

when the dawn would come
fires raced to the skies
veterans told stories
to steady the nerves
of the young ones

kâ-mônahihkos, Digging Weasel
ê-kî-nêhiyawatâmot
sang his Cree song
called his helper
kinêpik, snake
dug into earth
created a pathway through the earth
tunnel snuck past Blackfoot lines
emptied the camp
ê-pê-sâkâstêk
when the dawn would come
left the Blackfoot no one to fight

a boy was in a travois
wood cut earth
makes marks
tâpiskôc nêhiyawasinahikêwin
Cree writing, syllabics
pulled from sun
paths opened up
sun falls through new cracks
nâpêsis with *ohkoma*
passing through prairie
travois holding baby body
lost in paths of distant voices

boy was found
by a *môsâpêw*
buffalo bull
his old body cut
paths across prairie
full of clustered memories
sun's passing
he sheltered the boy
from the wind
sâpowâstan
blowing through

another bull
younger challenged him
did not want
the orphan boy in the camp
he came from those who
killed the buffalo, he said
they fought, raced
and the old buffalo won
kept the boy, sheltered him
a tree hiding the earth
from open suspicious sky

as time gathered
created words
and lost others
the boy was told
he had to go home
mosôm buffalo gave stories
holding memory
his body moving
ê-waskawît

people in the boy's camp
knew he was coming back
awa ê-kî-kosâpahtahk
performed the ceremony
opened ground and sang songs
he came back, came home
but as he left
grandfather buffalo
turned into stone

told him
reminded him
all he taught him
when the boy went back
he was made a leader
he left offerings at the stone
where grandfather laid
just like *kôkôcîs* left
food for *wîhtikôhkân*
stories and names are food
helps keep the life force
waskawîwin flowing

Buffalo Child
I remember
when you came to me
vulnerable, shy
unprotected from prairie wind
sickly, dry pasty skin
tired of open spaces
valley loses shelter
trees wind
through the end

Buffalo Child, *paskwâw-mostos*
wakes the prairie grass
promises of his grandfather
you give your hide
your house of being
sit on open prairie
heavy and old standing earth
broken by dynamite
tears the line of old relationship
but the ancient stone
becomes my body

Buffalo Child
paskwâw-mostos
rock has fallen
clipped from valley's embrace
but the story lives through
this boy
his body becomes
this ancient stone

our bodies tattooed
with land's memories
with land speak, *askîwêwin*
even though the stone is gone
the story lives on
old stories give our bodies shape
and guide the path of sound
like trees guiding the wind

MOSÔM GABRIEL'S FIGHT

Gabriel was not
the kind of man
who would back
down from a fight
he carried the beach
with him all of his days
he went to Debden
close to where he lived
went to town
lots of French people
mistikôsiwak
people of the wooden ships
like *cikôsiw*
who took treaty
from James Smith

he walked along the streets
buzzing with cars
farmers driving combines
you never saw
that on the Autobahn

there was another man
big, cocky
full of spit and vinegar
he looked at Gab
challenging him
asking him why he was in town
but Gab did not back down
looking him in the eye
they moved toward each other
in the space
sky closed in
sun hid in shadows

they danced around
fists whirling
the guy's hands
were really white now
usually he was just pink

Gab was not that tall
but he was the toughest man around
my dad told me
he was like Maximus
the Roman General from Spain
who fought the Germans
just like Gab
he had a heart the size of a Mac truck
and the arms of Hercules

he circled him
around and around
a shark circling
a struggling swimmer
he danced and dodged
played cat and mouse with him

he felt his stomach tighten
like he was hungry
not the same hungry
as the winter of 44-45
ispîhk ê-kî-kipahikâsot
when he was captured
but still hungry
he motioned
for the other man
to take a break
to rest, to pause
to catch their breath
took inventory

of his motions
of his moves
the other guy
was like a swimmer
struggling for dear life
like a third-party manager
trying to sort out the mess
running out of time
he was like a man
running for chief
with no close relatives
he needed more
he needed an angle
so he motioned for them
to take a break

they sat there
ate pork and beans
let me tell you
there's nothing like pork and beans
they had lemonade
to wash it down
nothing like lemonade
to wash the stuff down
they ate, prayed,
and toasted each other
then they continued to fight
till the end of the day
Gab was happy
just to dance around

MISTAHI-MASKWA, SONG ONE

kayâs mîna mistahi-maskwa
tracked traces in ground
to the edge of water
mistahi-maskwa kâ-kî-itiht
the one called *mistahi-maskwa*
bear claw around his neck
booming voice
twisting echo
ê-kâh-kistawêt
brought sleeping thunder
from under
nipiy kâ-pitihkwêk
to the sky

brave and generous
former *okihcitâw*
"put others before yourself"
"give away freely"
powers from others for others
mistahi-maskwa gave horses
gathered wind
from all directions
as his mount
pounded the earth
in small quick motions
would fly across the plains
he made his voice
cause the water
at *nipiy kâ-pitihkwêk*
to stand to the sky
brought thunderbirds
from the bottom of the lake
when he told Big Tall White Man
the Queen can never replace
kâ-miyikowisiyâhk
"what the Creator has given us"
kihci-okimâskwêw, Queen
also means
"old woman
with many relatives"
like the earth
which provides

MISTAHI-MASKWA, SONG THREE

ê-mâyahkamikahk
"where it went wrong"
that is how we say
the Northwest Rebellion
Treaties stripped of honour
old, heavy voices
fall from the written script
buffalo bones
become dry and chalky
melt into the earth
with calming slow rain
near Loon Lake
the army approached
Big Bear's camp
they say there was
a left-handed shooter
from Hobbema
who was a scout
the army opened fire
stripping light
from old men and old women

MISTAHI-MASKWA, SONG FOUR

"môy ê-nôhtê-sakâpêkinikawiyân," itwêw
"I don't want to
be pulled like a horse," he said
cool prairie wind blows through
sâpowâstan, creates new spaces
between trees
reshapes water
in new ways
old hunters fall
to planted ground
buffalo chased
by slow moving cattle

Old Ones saw ahead
he knew what was coming
ê-kiskiwêhikêt
ê-mamâhtâwisit
he was spiritually powerful
and shared his gifts
with the people

CÎHCAM

cîhcam, mother of Gabriel
cîhcam, daughter of *masaskâpaw*
"toes touching the bottom of the water"
my uncle Burton Vandall told me
water never leaving the sight of sky
cîhcam niece of *atâhkakohp*
Star Blanket, one of the chiefs
of the *wâskahikaniyiniwak*, House People

cîhcam, her body was our blanket
gave us life and language
brought stars from the sky
brought our souls from deep oceans
to the water of our birth
cîhcam was *mosôm* Gabriel's mother
cîhcam was grandmother to us all

there is a book written
blue binding and loose stiching
about her uncle *atâhkakohp*
the northern Star Blanket
from around Prince Albert
maps of kinship
connecting lines
name her as "unknown daughter"
but we know her as *kôkom cîhcam*

cîhcam did not take treaty
êkâ ê-akimiht, "not counted"
not counted by treaty

some of our relatives lived by *wâskîsiw*
hunting ground
place of rest in the world
lived in bush
trademarked now as a park

Grey Owl chased out Indians
to save the beaver
movie-reel Indians
chase real Indians
from folds of lakes
and curves of bush

land becomes heavy
with new words
old stories become distant
quiet whispers in tired mouths
new names fill the trees
game laws cut trap lines
iron tracks pass over
hunter's sleep

wind across the body
dries my cracking limbs
heavy like trees
can no longer trace the stars
nor bring the water to the sky
old names become cold whispers
our mouths
can no longer speak
old name memories

cîhcam, her words and stories
raise the earth through her lips
ancient poetic pathways
under her kitchen table
thrown blanket over
put rocks on skillet floor
improvised ceremony

cîhcam gave back air to lungs
sun back to sky
bring sanctuary of stories
and thick Cree poems
she is our blanket
of stars, takes us
to the edge of words
and the beginning of songs

we are her living body
storytellers and poets
hold traces of her
echoes and songs
give form
to the moments of our birth
warm us
with blankets of stars
wake sleeping water
to the sky

A FALSE RIVER

I used to pour vodka
into the empty spaces
of my soul
the holes eat at my skin
my flesh, my body, my vessel
is broken my spirit has no place
to touch the waking place of earth

my soul is translucent
shimmering with the water of vodka
but empty water
cannot house my soul
my body full of alcohol
becomes a false river

I remember I used to drink
through the days
the emptiness ate away at me
consumed all of my gentle memories
nôhkom washing my body
in the skin, heavy blue

I remember the gentle place
of the *matotisân*
the smell of sprinkled cedar
tullies soaked with water
alcohol kills me
and those quiet places
of Gabriel's beach
fade from my awareness
as I lose myself
in this false water

MOSÔM'S AID

when I felt sick and dying I wanted more
words failed me, as my body and lips became numb
I felt my body in this moment ache for movement
I lamented these small moments
felt darkness move into me
slowly with each moment
taking away light

I remembered the story
of my grandfather Gabriel
when he was in prison
and was in the earth
like a pit, and how he was forced
to eat mice to live
my sickness was like the pit
hidden and sunken in the earth
the only things that gave me comfort
were *nikos*
and the warmth of the *matotisân*

LOST

I remember the days
crushed and hollowed out
drained of all love and light
my father taught me
the rage of Gabriel's beach

crushing blows
bodies against walls
crushed bones
pleas of a wounded creature
begging for mercy
but receiving none

those moments wrap around me
and give me my place
in the world
and give me
my words

gentle voice of my son
brings me back
from false river dreams
to my house
all quiet words
and gentle whispers tear
the darkness
take the orange
from the sky of a setting sun

as men, we all lost our way
unable to find the paths
that guided ancestors
helped make them
good and honourable

I kissed my son
my empty fists
had frightened
his mother
the world around me
had fallen from the sky

I lost my body
I could no longer
carry sound
my dry and brittle bones
unable to hold
old *kayâs* ago memories

I remember her crying
like my mother
I had become my father's son
I could feel the fire
of Gabriel's beach
move through my body
and fingers

I reached out
but her body turned to sand
losing form
I fell deeper into the darkness
I knew I was truly lost

I am forever the son
of a lost river
holding sand
from Gabriel's beach
on a dry shore
with no *mêmêkwêsiwak*
to sculpt my body and soul
back into a whole form
I am scattered in small pieces
on a bloody beach

MY CHILDHOOD

I realize now that all of those things
left empty oceans in my soul
no cool winds
bringing pieces
of warm sun's dream
could ever fill
the holes in the water

my body was my beach
empty of stories
and old voices
after time I fall back
into the great silence
of the dead water
that consumes my soul
piece by piece
I pray to the Great Mystery
in small stillness

Ê-KÎ-PÊ-KÎWÊYÂN ITÊ KÂ-TIPISKÂK
I COME HOME TO THE DARKNESS

the darkness hollowed
out the light from my eyes
and the warmth from my heart

took me to deepest dreams
sun made no marks
on the earth of my flesh
only blackness covers
the light of my marrow

I find comfort in this cold place
away from light
wrapped in blankets of earth
I think of my grandfather Gabriel
when he was captured and
taken away from the sun
from the laughter of friends
from the thoughts
and memories of rivers
parklands and hills
he found his death to be slow
and measured like a *wîhtikow*

opening the blood from dry bones
springing lost wetness to his lips
I lay in this darkness
make myself home
like my grandfather Gabriel

Sons of a Lost River

....

MÊMÊKWÊSIWAK TREE

they spoke of little people
apisciyinîsak, the *mêmêkwêsiwak*
môy ê-okoticik
"They didn't have noses"
about three feet tall
little people waited by the tree
iskwâhtêm, the door
my *mosôm* said
old people would
dream of this place
maskihkiy, bits of earth and plants
given to dreamers

mêmêkwêsiwak were healers
faces etched in rock
by the door
they would give small pouches
and ribbons, *sênipânak*
given the medicine
the little people were healers

an old Swede saw them
standing by water
under a pale heavy moon
ê-kî-wâsakâmêkâpawicik
stood in a circle
and made songs
with their ancient water drums

old *pâcinîs* surveyed
divided up the land
like a dealer divides up cards
found one of the little people
ê-kî-pôni-waskawît
who had stopped moving
an old man
told him to put it back
in a little box
hidden in the clay of earth

doorway, treeway
doors of dreams
are pine trees
mêmêkwêsiwak, the little ones
came to old dreamers
and gave them gifts from *askiy*

there is a tree
where these beings came from
dried at root
arms without skin and fingers
branches hold nothing
but an empty sky

they say, Charles Burns told me,
when the tree dies
the earth is poisoned
and will die too

SONS OF A LOST RIVER

I.

ancient pathway river
guided old travellers
kisiskâciwan, fast flowing river
our dreams
catch the sun
in small moments
memory falls forever
water passes river path
becomes old and quiet

my sons, you wander
in land empty of echoes
without ancient songs
you will be sons
of a lost river
unable to find
your home
on any beach

II.

we carry Gabriel's beach
within us
carry lost fire
pieces of days
stretched too far
to hold colour and texture

shells exploded over
water, dark and heavy
from a lost river unrelenting
ocean fails to open

I remembered the small boy
whose small hands
lifted me from the water
near Gabriel's beach
now that water has dried
and my skin burns
from the metal shells

I felt the chamber, deadened
threads of memory unravel
loosened of their colour

III.

I grew up near the forks
of the Saskatchewan River
which I can no longer find

at Batoche where some
of my grandfathers fought
so that we could live with dignity
Gabriel's uncle Joseph
buried outside of the church
in sight of river lost

I remembered the prayers
of orange thunderbirds
guided past sounding waters
that took me past
pits of captivity
deep, sunken earth

I thank you *mosôm* Gabriel
for giving me stories
to help me find the still
places of the beach

I pull massed form
from my heart
from my chest
bury the bullets
from *mosôm*'s gun
find my way
back to the sky

I dreamt of these things
as the first light of day
hit my body
my throat was dry
needing water
from a lost river

IV.

I remember dreaming water
seeing old men in rifle pits withdrawing
scarred and fractured earth
from their bodies
to save a river
which gave the water
to their souls

we would forever be
sons of a lost river
a river that had lost its way
and wandered through
old sleeping valleys
hollowed water
no longer shaped
by the wind of dreams

bus stretches metal body
on road through thick forest
big glasses, hair like Beethoven
his words meet many closed eyes
reluctant to open to idle chatter

"Hey sweetheart,
do you want my Big Mac?"
says the old macked out Mack
he staggers his way
through English lines
French rhythms creep through
scattered words in a scattered story
water soothes cold winter roads
trees thick hold the cover and night

"Doctor says I have
to smoke for my heart"
"I was framed"
smoke from the bathroom
woman coughs and complains
to the bus driver
Old Beethoven hair
yells at her
"Damn bitch"
young men rise
to challenge
old rooster's call

they say further north by Timmins
if you stop on the highway
put your hand in front of your face
darkness will eat all light
"You Jesus haters"
Hitler salute
mumbles in Czech
he lights his cigarette again

bus driver gets up
tells him the OPP are coming
to greet him at
Blind River
I grow blind
headlights cut the darkness
into small bits
make the night bearable

SPRING TIME IN KINISTINO

my dad and Edwin Tootoosis
were telling stories
about *wîhtikôhkân* and the traveler
rednecks tried to chase us out
with their hard, long stares
we finished our meal
eggs rolls, rice and coffee

miyoskamihk, the spring
breaking ice filled the air
rebirth of possibilities
turning of eternity
penetrated the space around us
creating calmness
trucks in half-filled streets

my dad told a story
an old man and his grandson
went to town piled in a truck
to get groceries
the boy was fourteen

they milled about the store
collected the things they needed
filled their carts
there was a man at the door
he said, "Goddamn Indians."
spoke to the old man
"You are Goddamn lazy.
Stay on the reserve."
taunts, and mean red faces
from red necks
old man kept calm
they gathered their groceries

by the truck
the grandson asked,
"*nimosôm* (my grandfather),
why didn't you say
something to the man who
was saying those things to us?"
The grandfather said,
"How long were we
in that store *nôsisim*?"
"Five minutes"
"We only had to deal
with that man
for five minutes
he has to deal with himself
for the rest of his life."

PINE TREE

Treaty traces
land with cold metal
in our fingers
trying to find
the fire and places
trees give us shelter
and hold together
the spaces of days

the late Jim Kâ-Nîpitêhtêw
pimwêwêhahk
"sound of a constant drumming"
make the old tree sing
"there was this body
that needed someone," *itwêw*
spruce trees stand
on old treaty ground

he says
"I guess that this
was the one that
was placed in this body," *itwêw*
shell of being
they sat on the ground
bright green grass
pale blue shirt
scattered black
the sound to one point
my *mosôm* spoke
a loud clear voice

he pointed to the tree
"When the spruce stands up
and meets you
it meets you with dignity
because he has lived his life
the way he was placed here," *itwêw*
tree marker of life, of being
dry, the bright summer sun
stretches to the ground
"Everyone of us is beautiful.
We should leave our bodies
with dignity," *itwêw*

old *pimwêwêhahk*
had adopted *nimosôm*
as his son
and my *mosôm*
housed some
of *pimwêwêhahk*'s being

DREAMS OF AN OPEN FIELD

I dreamt of slow rivers
that move
through my flesh
deep dreams of water
like old Cree hunters
I want to find
the creatures of my soul
in your body
your lips show me their paths
I long to see your eyes
to share slow, secret kisses
to move to the deep water
of deep oceans

sky turning orange
fragments of day
falling with the sun
on its descent
my feet
crunched harvested wheat
path uncertain
whole landscape
spread in all directions
trees on the perimeter
outlining the stretch
of the field on two sides
I walked for a long time
as the sun's light collapsed
when I awoke
I only found
empty spaces
which had held
your lips
and quiet spaces
which had sheltered
your words

PIPON

winter wind
cold breath
on my back
water cracks
snap of ice
old words reborn
die on the surface
of my skin, orange
passing sky
into the earth
shelter to poems
that hedge
on the hinterland
sky becomes
heavy and earth
my lips cold

my limbs
become dry
and crack
against the wind
unable to hold movement
my heart closes
contracts and falls
into the earth
thin stretching
limbs of ice
numb, without feeling
or path

LONG WINTER

the snow falls and falls
a blanket of cold
in a winter
which never ends
I have dug my way
out of so many holes
this hole seems so deep
I feel my hands becoming blue
away from you
my sensation fades
no longer feeling

WAL-MART HUSTLE

Wal-Mart jungle
cheap capitalist safari
brings back the trophy
white women
with fake nails
Indian women
with dyed perms
Indian men
with white women
old man smiles
he found his buffalo
in bargain bin deals
wallet pulled
bills become loose
he waits the applause of
the clerk
as she notes his bargain
he looks around for approval
I wondered why
Osama wanted to kill
this glorious dream

TRIBUTE TO BOB BARKER

a tip of the headdress
to the greatest
Indian showman of all time
Bob Barker, Bob the barker
barking out
numbers, gave us hope
gave democracy hope
in a time of great darkness

showed us that Osama
could not *osâmihêw*
do too much
he showed us
that the spinning wheel
could still inspire a nation

the way he looked
at those ladies
with their blue hair
while they spun the wheel
they could "come on down"

like a powwow announcer
Bob cried out
gave us hope
and made us believe

he always reminded us
to have our rez dogz spaded
or neutered
thanks Bob
for the memories
and the laughs

THANK YOU MR. BRAD PITT

thank you Mr. Brad Pitt
I salute you sir
you get her juiced up
and loosed up
butter her bannock
bingo card ready

thank you Mr. Brad Pitt
I take my best baby
she watches you
on the flicker show
she follows your muscle line
with her hem lines

thank you Mr. Brad Pitt
Thelma and Louise
young, buck strutting
six pack sculpture
Achilles berserker
climbs walls of Troy
pushes the sanctuary
she wants you to climb
her walls

my lover gets hot
like a Coleman stove
at a powwow
thank you Mr. Brad Pitt
for making my Mrs. Smith
burn her apple pie

paperwork is set up
batter on deck
well I got to say
the car is tanked
warm inside
bannock is torn open
like my pantz

I think of you and me
Mr. Brad Pitt
as a team
like Ocean's Two
just me and you

THE BALLAD OF BAYNE SIMON

kayâs long time ago
when the first bannock
was cooling
parkland colours stretched
to the rounding
of the world's corner
like one of *nôhkom*'s quilts
Bayne Simon
put black lines
on that quilt

he had a bike
called "Green Machine"
tassels like a Vegas show girl
twisted on his hands
shine caught
the sheen of the sun
rode like a chopper
and he was Peter Fonda
looking for adventure
with his Fanta orange bottle
duct taped to the side

his dad worked at the Co-op
open shirts
spoke in rehearsed aphorisms
like "Time is money"

Bayne did what few others
ever did in their whole lives
when he was only ten
I can hear
"The Ride of the Valkyries"
playing in the background
he moved through space
like the great Harlem Globetrotters
who had come out to our school

he challenged the Grim Reaper
to a game of rock, paper, scissors
on that long parkland road
and won

his feet digging
deeper and deeper
to the floor of awareness
grounded parklands
he kept going
had a sip
from his orange Fanta
from the bottle
and tried to put the metal cap
back on
fumbled as he kept
peddling and peddling
his feet to the road
cap fell, slipping from his grasp

he rode up the hill
you could see for miles
Red Deer Hill
an old deer was there
before the reserve time
could hear everything
for hundreds of miles
with his large antlers
like a CB radio

he dug deeper
than a chief
into the band till
deep in his heart
he found the strength
he passed over the hill
and could see us all
waving back at him in Kinistino
he lifted himself to the sky
with his feet
his young, thin legs
shaking like trees in a storm
but holding together
he made it up the hill
his story happened 27 years ago
but I still remember his ballad

POWWOW LEGEND

urban neechi
in his doubt
leaky of ancient rhyme
but not a mariner
wanting to hear
kayâs school stories
to fill unstoried ear

"I will tell you a legend
to the yout' from Regina"
the powwow announcer pops
like pieces of bread
out of a toaster
"we are all here
because of brave people," *itwêw*

he tells the story
padlocks on doors
10 years ago
(but it was really 13 years ago
not good with numbers)
his story goes into
third party management

casino chips
are today's buffalo chips
naughty li'l Nanabush smiles
gives up his wandering ways
settles down
with a wife
and kids

the storyteller talks
powwow commercials
"my brother has a job now"
"my cousin works security"

urban neechi
hears old rhyme
without reason

POWWOW MORNING

seagull cries good morning
"mommy is that a bird singing"
spices and spouses
laid out in tents and teepees
young people wake
up the sleeping road
tell stories of 49ers
turned to 69ers
possible hook-ups
and gangsta shake-downs
tarps rustle in the wind
quick snaps
dry sun opens day
bright yellow
powwow breakfast
couples smile
trying to hold
their relationships together
like Han Solo and the Falcon
toast with heavy butter
coffee dark and thick
makes the air powwow
I see *mosôm's* name
nimosôm owîhowin
on security guard back
guitar slung on back
Young Johnny Cash
tries the early morning sounds

"she was patting the seat"
he motions
seagulls give movement to sky
flies pretend the top of the tent
is heaven
and Young Johnny
pretends to be
powwow's angel

JAMES SMITH HOCKEY ARENA

we took our slough
to the Big Arena
bright lights
bleachers filled
fried gravy soaked
sugar candy
in our hands
diabetes starter kits

buffalo and moose calls
become cat calls
to brave white kids
who came to play
in our hood

bleachers gone now
dark inside
pockets of light
breaking through
like parkland nights
sky holds dark blue
like deep ocean
around me

Gretzky's retired now
I haven't skated in years
when I saw the arena
in recent times
wannabe neechi hustlers
stories on the wall
Crips and Bloods
in south-central James Smith

young reznecks
stretch the necks
of their rez stories
like giraffes
and make old men
dream of prime
neechi alphabet soup

old place scaffolds
bodies empty of motion
some places on ice
never froze
now the memories
pass from this old
hulled out body
of memory building

CASINO CULTURE

Buffalo Bill would be happy
we sell cultural ass
to make patriot Americans
comfortable with Manifest Destiny
and imperial machinations
the powwow trail

white people
make themselves feel good
about the conquest of America
and the destruction of Indigenous memory
by marvelling at "all of the regalia"
"and are you really Sioux?"
cheap chokers
made from Wal-Mart merchandise
they eat their little bits
of ancient America
make themselves fat
on authentic neechi bannock

the casino lords
over the landscape
contemporary neechi temple
gaudy powwow colours
lime green and neon orange
Vegas meets neechiness
poker tables take the place of old stories
old campfires become neon

white men play Indian
speak of their wolf dreams
wait anxiously for grand entry
but where the hell were they in 1885
when it wasn't cool to be a neechi?

YOUR BODY HOLDS THE FLIGHT OF MY SOUL

your kisses take me
beyond the latitudes of
nitahcahkom
your body maps
the journey
to find the lost river

I kiss you from a great lonely hunger
only your tongue
can move to speak away
your tongue on mine
slow touch, like lonely birds
in great blue sky
coming together
to feel the flight of the other

your hands opened
nitahcahkom
from a great sleep
a fractured gentleness
hidden far in my dreams
scarred skin becomes alive again
as you held me
you held ancient stars
that could never end

I heard something above
fly quickly, a burst of movement
cut the empty space, gave it form
I wondered what soul this movement held
inside of you
I dreamt the secrets
of a lost river
touched the earth of your skin
to find my way home

nicâpân kôkôcîs spoke many things
told tales of many telling
GWG work shirts
heavy black Indian Affairs glasses
brown fingers move the still
ground around him
with heavy stories
that shift slowly from the ground
like sleeping horses

kôkôcîs spoke of *maci-maskihkiy*
bad medicine in the *kayâs* ago days
people scared one another
power used to draw lines
created fear
manufactured respect
unravels threads of community

propaganda smiling faces fell
fill annual reports
everything is fine they say
the Indian mafia
"Fire? What do you mean?"
"Don't worry it's just
bannock gone wrong"

black leather jackets
shiny rings
Indian mafia
like the Taliban
tries to control a truth
destroys threads of community
money, *sôniyâw*
gives power
eats our compassion
like a *wîhtikow*

NEECHI TALIBAN

"Taliban, Taliban, bannock and bananas"
more lies come
and me wan' go home

"Kiss the ring" "Kiss the ring"
that 'chi man say
black leather jackets
move and kinda sway
grab dem thinking boxes
and open dem up
"We fight for de people"
the 'chi Chief say

come relatives, come kinfolk
come around
eat ya fill from the trough
while you can
he be handin' out da jobs
and da bannock too
like today's Indian Agent man
but he be kinda brown

"Taliban, Taliban, bannock and bananas"
selfish government come
and me wan' go home

KÂH-KAYÂS SÎPIY MÔSKICIWAN KIYAWIHK OHCI
ANCIENT RIVER MOVES AGAIN FROM YOUR BODY

I.

I am forever a son of a lost river
kâ-pâstêkamipayik, dried water
forever, shimmering translucent dream
of a forever earth, *kâkikê-askiy*
becomes solid and fixed
old Cree dreamers
can no longer dream
in this empty, dry place

I remember when I was a young boy
I searched for sanctuaries
but found none
long deep sleeps
became morning
gently on my body
with the whispers of birds
piyêsîsak ê-kîmwêcik
letting the day ride down to my soul
through their wings

my throat opened to greet the sky
but a dark mucous
filled its remembrance
I could make no sound
as the sky became darker
birds could not hear
my cry for the sky, my call for shelter
my body became numb
blood in my marrow
became dry and brown
a dead, dry river

II.

nikî-wâpâsin, I awoke in early morning
to try to remember
the suns old, *kayâs* ago promises
my body, *niyaw*, the house of my soul
and the windows of my being warm slowly
your golden brown skin is my sun, *nipîsim*,
your fingers are the gentle blue skies
of old *kayâs* ago days and your eyes
rivers flowing deep and strong
your lips open the sky
to the sound of old bird songs

your water moves old bones of old beings
your thighs hold fields of wild sweet flowers
winding through your hips
kâ-waskawi-sîpiy, moving energy in river
forest stretch of your legs ends
surrounds me, and I feel
the ancient warmth of the first dawn

I feel your warm tears
your honey scent opens my skin
to the ceremonies of ancient water
your eyes open the dark places of my dreams
fill my soul with forgotten river songs
upon the surface
of a waking earth

SÎPÎSIS

she spoke of *sîpîsis*, little river
where she would go
away from the dark shadows
cast by an unforgiving sun
she found the water
to give her comfort
give her still places
in her waking dreams
her hands opened
promises of water
her eyes closed
and she moved
through her dreams

êkwa mîna ê-kî-pawâtât
nâpêwa ôtê nîkânihk
she dreamt of a man
who would be her *sîpîsis*
whose arms would be
like the trees along its stretch
whose love
would forever warm her soul

she in turn became a great river
that could dream back
the water of a dry land
helped a son of a lost river
find his way home forever

DREAMS OF OLD CREE HUNTERS

I think of the slow rivers moving through my flesh
where I dream deep dreams of deep water
like old Cree hunters, I want to find the creatures
of my soul in your body, your lips show me their paths
behind the roads of their creation and play
I long to see your eyes, to share slow, secret kisses
to move to the deep water
of deep oceans, lose my thoughts
and fall into the hidden spaces of days

BATTLE OF OLDMAN RIVER

they built Fort Whoop-Up
where the last great Indian battle
happened 100 years before I was born
in your love, I have built a new fort
in your body, I have a new vantage point
see new patterns

along the far ridge, the Cree
expecting victory move toward
the camps of their enemies
as I have moved through darkness
so they did toward dawn

my life has been a battle
like many of the old Crees
I have died in crimson water
crushed by the power of dark horses
betrayed by dawn's calling

they met fierce resistance from the south
blows from the darkness
like those of my dreams
they died in coulees,
I die in my dreams
when I am away from you

imagine their long trek home
wounded tired bodies
the dry sun
peeling the marrow
from their bones
as they journeyed home

I have found my home
in your light, your body,
your prayers, and kisses

I dreamt of long passages colours in the day stretched
but still recognizable and available to the reference
points in my mind. I run faster faster run through my
body my hands open trying to catch its pathway. My
mouth opens to anticipate places of rest. My legs carry
me through each moment pounding the space between
the centre of my being in the earth. I feel the eyes upon
me always chasing always aware. The *wîhtikow* whispers
in my ear telling me secrets of a deep darkness that lies
below the surface of all things. Secrets tell me to lay
down lay still and let the eyes see my soul. I am tired
my lungs are empty of breath. My body cannot run any
more. My soul can no longer hold the whispers of
darkness. My hands form a solid mass. Fisted. I turn
and look up the hill. A man stands there.

He left his car and reached for a cigarette. His suit
caught the sun in different moments moving the light
like water hitting my eyes and causing me to turn away.
I walked up to him and noticed he looked like myself.
Same energy same pace of movement but I could not
see behind his sunglasses. I reached for a gun to kill
me. I pushed my body to the ground shifting my
position. I got up and peered through my cover on the
hard cement and shot him. He died quickly. I went to
the woman beside him. She had brown bronzy skin.
She was dressed very well. Her dress was red or orange
and it caught her collar bone at two points draping
from the back and front. I grabbed her slowly and the
blood from mine caught her hands. I kissed her and she
kissed me. Old memories broke the surface of quietude
and solitude that had held them. Her love warmed my
soul my dry lips became wet again and my hands could
stretch to the sky. Sky moving through her became calm
and peaceful.

WORD MAP FOR LOST SONS

our words come from land and places
our stories are echoes
of the land of our ancestors
clusters of sound become our bodies
before language, we had songs
ancient songs that shook the land
like *piyêsîsak kâ-naskwêwahamawâcik pîsimwa*
the birds answering the sun in song
as the old Cree song says
all sound and language
comes from this original thank you

nôtokwêw âtayôhkan
the keeper of all sacred stories
âtayôhkêwina
the keeper of ancient sound
and our helper and grandmother
kikâwînaw-askiy k-ôkwêmêsit,
the late Beatrice Lavallee
spoke of these things

she said *nôtokwêw âtayôhkan*
these words we must remember
nihtâwêwin
to speak well
to choose our words carefully
to guide our sons with love and not anger
to speak pure love to our lovers
to speak our hearts open

tâpwêwin, truth
to be guided by old principles
of the *okihcitâwak*
to protect and honour our women
to speak truth and not lies
to love one woman and blanket her
with the original thank-you song of the universe
from the wet throats of birds
who sang the sun into the first day

THE FIRE IS MY GIFT

sometimes I think of those days
of that old house
sometimes I want to drink
I used to want to punch things,
walls, anything

I have to control it
but my anger
the fire of Gabriel's beach
saved my life

it got me off the ground
like where the old woman
lay in the field, falling on her
ready to die
my anger,
the fire of Gabriel's beach
saved my life

MY BODY BECOMES RIVER AGAIN

I fall past things
winter dreams
old words reborn
and die
on the surface
of my skin
I pass from sky
to earth
I lay close
to a passing sun
surface of my being orange
desire grows cold
under winter cover
my heart held
my body's warmth
opened like a flower
universe soaks through
cold blue of winter sky passes
hears the forgotten whispers
of small animals
who gather plants
bring limbs of forgotten trees
attach them to my heart
space of the earth opens again
small animals
catch the warmth of open fires
in their open mouths
bring back
breath of earth bound stars
bring water from distant rivers
moisten my failing dry flesh
becomes *kisiskâciwan*

Words for My Sons

....

WORDS FOR MY SONS

My sons, we are all, lost sons of a lost river. We have lived our lives in the shadows of thunderbirds. Our name bears their trace through the sky, *nîkân-isi*, the foremost being, but we live away from them. We have been dragged to the bottom of water, pulled into a space without colour and form, a place without ancestral memories. We have anger, but we no longer have the honour of the old *okihcitâwak*.

His anger was like *iskotêw*, fire, a rage that burned through all skin, all flesh, and made the house weak. The poison made the river of our ancestors black, heavy with unhealthy form and rotted the marrow of our skin

I remember when I was five, my head burned, my body sweated, and my fingers reached for water, but, like Gabriel on the beach, they could not find form, only the empty spaces of stories, empty sound without words. I saw monsters, blobs, chunks of colour, green, orange, vibrating, electric pulse crash through walls, and yell at me. I imagine how my *mosôm* Gabriel experienced the same forms crashing into him on the beach. It was there that I began to dream of *wîhtikow*. Later in my life, I could name this darkness, this hallowing of the house as *wîhtikow*.

nikosisitik, my sons, I speak of these things to you because I love you, and I want your life to be guided by old thunderbirds. I want you to find the river again, the river of our ancestors that flows through your bodies. I want the house of memories, the house of old stories to be calm and still in your lives. I want your body to be full of heavy, blue, vibrant water. Through your lives, the river can be found again.

We are sons of a lost river. The only way we can find our way back to this river is to be honest about the past. Not only about how we have been hurt, but how we have hurt others. We must also question how we became lost, how we lost our way.

nikosisitik, you have seen these things and have heard them. Understand that we have become sons of a lost river. Understand how we became violent and lost. I urge you to speak of these things. Our women have been strong in their stories, but we have been weak in our silence. Remember, it is our grandmothers who helped us survive.

I remember how my house was like that body of my father's house and I remember when alcohol became a false river. I was lost, without anchor, without stories, naked in the middle of a great silence. The ancient river was so dry in my soul that I could no longer cry.

I remember when she stayed out all night, drinking, away, I watched our son. She had deserted me, my misery, and my anger. I had brutalized her spirit and I had hurt her body. My words were like a poison that ate away at her soul. They were like a virus that changed her love to darkened poisoned water. Closed in my tired, forgetting sky, I hurt her physically, and I am sorry that I was not strong enough to hold the fire of Gabriel's beach with grace.

I realized, at that moment, I had truly become my father's son, a bearer of his anger. I realized my hands were not strong enough to hold the fire of Gabriel's beach. I was part of a chain that stretched to the past, a darkened legacy which had its roots in ê-mâyahkamikahk "where it went wrong" 1885.

To save ourselves, our families, and our communities, we need to find our way back to *kisiskâciwani-sîpiy* the Saskatchewan River, the river of our language, of our ceremonies, and of our honour.

I have heard in the old days, the *okihcitâwak* would deal severely with any man who hit his wife. The old *okihcitâwak* measured their lives by the ideas of bravery, courage, and selflessness. We need these things if we are to find the river within our bodies. I need to find my way back to the river like my father before me.

I remember her kind eyes warmed me. They were gentle, light from stretched hands, that caught small pieces of stars inside of her. We smoke outside. I smoked mine to the bone, and heard her stories speak. She told me she couldn't remember my name. She told me names were not important, it was what was inside of us, our hearts, our souls. Names were like a house, what gave the name life was what was inside, what was inside the house, the people, inside the way were relationships, respect, and dialogue. Words were like a body that gave a name flesh. Words and stories gave a name a place to rest, water to move, a space to create. Later that night, she prayed for our food at the meal, the place was full of energy, of laughter and people. She later presented me a drawing her son did of a thunderbird.

I thanked her as we smoked. She told me I was kind, and I told her my ancestor's name was Thunderbird, *nîkân-isi*, her story and words gave my name form.

Glossary of Cree Words and Phrases

apisciyinîsak: the little people

askiy: land, earth

askîhk: on the Earth, on the land

askîwêwin: the voice of the land, the land's voice

astotin: hat

atâhkakohp: Starblanket; Cree chief, signatory to Treaty Six

ati-pihkopayinwa nicihciya: my hands turn to ash

awa: this, this one

awa ê-kî-kosâpahtahk: this one foresaw it, the one that performed
the shaking tent ceremony

awâsis: child

âtayôhkêwina: sacred stories; spiritual history

cikôsiw: French Man (clipped from *(wê)miscikôsiw*)

cîhcam: Maria Vandall, my great-great-great-grandmother

ê-akimiht: he/she/it is counted

ê-akohkasikêt: he is welding

ê-ispipitahk: he pulls it up

ê-kâh-kistawêt: it echoes repeatedly

ê-kiskiwêhikêt: he foretells, he prophecies

ê-kî-kipahikâsot: he was captured, imprisoned

ê-kî-kosâpahtahk: he foresaw it, he performed the shaking tent
ceremony

ê-kî-nêhiyawatâmot: he was singing a Cree song

ê-kî-pawâtât: she dreamt of him

ê-kî-pê-kîwêyân itê kâ-tipiskâk: I came home to the darkness

ê-kî-pôni-waskawît: he had stopped moving, he had died

ê-kî-tapasît: he fled

ê-kî-wâsakâmêkâpawicik: they stood in a circle

ê-kîmwêcik: they are whispering

ê-mamâhtâwisit: he is spiritually powerful

ê-mâyahkamikahk: where it went wrong, the Northwest Resistance
of 1885

ê-osîhiht: he/she/it was made

ê-pê-sâkâstêk: coming dawn, dawn arrives

ê-tapasît: he flees

ê-waskawît: he is moving

ê-wî-pê-sâkâstêk: the sun is going to rise

êkâ: not

êkâ ê-akimiht: she was not counted, she was not enumerated under treaty

êkwa: and, then

êkwa mâmâsîs ê-osîhiht: and he/she/it was made poorly

êkwa mîna ê-kî-pawâtât nâpêwa ôtê nîkânihk: and she dreamt of a man in the future

iskotêw: fire; Burns, grandfather of Gabriel Vandall and my great-great-great-great-grandfather

iskoyikohk itê ê-kanawâpahtamân: as far as I look

iskwâhtêm: door

ispîhk: when, then

ispîhk ê-kî-kipahikâsot: when he was captured

ispîhk ê-wî-pê-sâkâstêk: when the sun is going to rise, when sunrise is imminent

itê kâ-tipiskâk: where it is dark

itwêw: he said, he said so, he said it

k-ôkwêmêsit: one who is named after another

kahkiyaw waniskâwak askîhk: everything on the Earth awakens, Mother Earth awakens

kayâs: long ago

kayâs mîna mistahi-maskwa: long ago also, Big Bear

kayâs-maci-maskihkiy: old time bad medicine

kâ-kî-itiht: who was called (by such a name) [referring to a deceased person]

kâ-miyikowisiyâhk: what the Creator has given us

kâ-mônahihkos: Digging Weasel

kâ-naskwêwahamawâcik: those who sing in response or accompaniment to him/her/them

kâ-pâstêkamipayik: the water which has dried up

kâ-pitihkwêk: that which rumbles, thuds

kâ-tipiskâk: where it is dark, the darkness; when it is dark

kâ-waskawi-sîpiy: moving energy river

kâh-kayâs sîpiy môskiciwan kiyawihk ohci: the ancient river flows forth from your body

kâkikê: forever

kâkikê-askiy: forever earth

kêtahtawê: suddenly, all of a sudden

kêtahtawê ê-kî-tapasît: suddenly he fled

kêtahtawê ê-tapasît: suddenly he flees

kihci-okimâskwêw: the Queen; old woman with many relatives

kikâwînaw-askiy: Mother Earth, our mother the Earth

kikâwînaw-askiy k-ôkwêmêsit: She who has Mother Earth as her Namesake, the late Beatrice Lavallee from Piapot First Nation

kinanâskomitin: thank you, I am grateful to you

kinêpik: snake

kinosêw: fish; brother of *wîhtikôhkân*

kisiskâciwan: it flows swiftly; the Saskatchewan River

kisiskâciwani-sîpiy: the swift-flowing river; the Saskatchewan River

kiyawihk ohci: from your body

kôhkom: your grandmother

kôkom: Grandmother! (address form); grandmother, respected older woman

kôkom cîhcam: grandmother *cîhcam*, Maria Vandall

kôkôcîs: Peter Vandall, my great-grandfather

maci-maskihkiy: bad medicine

masaskâpaw: Stands on the Bottom of the Water; my great-great-great-great-grandfather, father of *cîhcam*, Maria Vandall

maskihkiy: medicine

maskihkiy astotin: Medicine Hat

matotisân: sweat-lodge

mâmâsîs: poorly, any old way

mêmêkwêsiwak: the Little People

mistahi-maskwa: Big Bear

mistahi-maskwa kâ-kî-itiht: he who was called Big Bear

mistasiniy: big stone, large boulder

mistikôsiwak: people of the wooden boats, French people

miyoskamihk: the spring, in the spring

mîna: and, also

mosôm: grandfather; Grandfather! (address form)

mosôm Gabriel: grandfather Gabriel Vandall, my great-great-grand-uncle (in the English kinship system), *pâcinîs'* younger brother

mosôm pâcinîs: grandfather *pâcinîs* (Patrice adapted for Cree sound system); Patrick Vandall, my great-great-grandfather

mostos: cow, buffalo; brother of *wîhtikôhkân*

môhcw-âyak: crazy ones, foolish ones

môsâpêw: man who gives his life for others (old interpretation of the word), single male, unattached buffalo bull

môskiciwan: it flows forth

"môy ê-nôhtê-sakâpêkinikawiyân," itwêw: I don't want to be lead by a rope (like a horse) he said

môy ê-okoticik: they don't have noses

môya: no

napocokan: crooked hips; Bernard Constant, my great-great-great-grandfather

nâpêsis: boy, small boy

nâpêw: man

nêhiyawak: Crees, Cree people

nêhiyawasinahikêwin: Cree writing, Cree Syllabics

nicâpân: my great-grandparent

nicâpân kôkôcîs: my great-grandfather *kôkôcîs*; Peter Vandall

nicihciya: my hands

nihtâwêwin: speaking well, fluency

nikî-waniskân: I awoke, I arose

nikî-wâpâsin: I arose early; I was an early-riser

nikosis: my son

nikosisitik: my sons! (address form)

nimosôm: my grandfather

nimosôm owîhowin: my grandfather's name

nipahi-miyosit: terribly beautiful

nipiy: water

nipiy kâ-pitihkwêk: Sounding Lake, literally, "water which rumbles"

nipîsim: my sun

nitahcahkom: my spirit

niyaw: my body

nîkân-isi: the foremost one, Thunderbird; the first McLeod, my great-great-great-grandfather

nôhkom: my grandmother

nôsisim: my grandchild; my grandson, my granddaughter

nôtokwêw âtayôhkan: Grandmother Spirit; "old woman spirit being," keeper of language and sacred stories

ohci: from

ohkoma: his grandmother

okihcitâw: worthy young man, warrior

okihcitâwak: worthy young men, warriors

opakwahtêhon: his belt

opakwahtêhon ê-ispipitahk: he pulled up his belt

osâmihêw: he does too much with him/her/them

owîhowin: his/her name

ôtê nîkânihk: in the future

paskwâw-mostos: buffalo

paskwâw-mostos awâsis: Buffalo Child

pâcinîs: Patrick Vandall, my great-great-grandfather

pimwêwêhahk: "sound of a constant drumming"; Jim Kâ-Nîpitêhtêw

pipon: winter, it is winter

piyêsîsak: birds

piyêsîsak ê-kîmwêcik: the birds are whispering

piyêsîsak kâ-naskwêwahamawâcik pîsimwa: when the birds sing in response to the sun, birds which accompany the sun in song

pîsim: the sun

sâh-sîhcisiwak: they were packed together tightly

sâpowâstan: the wind blows through

sâpowâstêw: it shines through

sênipânak: ribbons

sîpiy: river

sîpîsis: stream, creek, rivulet, little river

sôniyâw: money

tâpiskôc: like, just as if

tâpiskôc nêhiyawasinahikêwin: like Cree writing, like Cree Syllabics

tâpwêwin: truth

timikamîhk: in deep water

waniskâwak: they arise, they awaken

waskawîwin: movement, life force

wâskahikaniyiniwak: the House People, division of the Cree who dwelt in the vicinity of Fort Carlton

wâskîsiw: Waskesiu, name derived from Woods Cree *wâwâskîsiw* "elk"

wîhtikow: a being who consumes other beings, cannibal, an ancient darkness

wîhtikowak: beings who consume other beings, cannibals

wîhtikôhkân: my great-great-great-grandfather, a Cree-Dene from the Cold Lake area of Alberta

Neal McLeod is a writer, visual artist, film-maker, comedian, and academic. He holds a doctorate in Interdisciplinary Studies, and currently teaches at Trent University in Peterborough, Ontario. He studied art in Sweden and has exhibited his unique and powerful paintings in galleries throughout Canada. His first book of poetry, *Songs to Kill a Wîhtikow* (Hagios, 2005), won the Aboriginal Poetry Book of the Year at the Anskohk Aboriginal Literature Festival in 2006. A serious scholar, he is also the author of *Cree Narrative Memory: From Treaties to Contemporary Times* (Purich Publishing, 2007). *Gabriel's Beach* is his second collection of poetry. He lives in Keene, Ontario, with his partner Tasha and two sons, Glen and Cody.